SYMBOLS OF THE UNITED STATES

Constitution

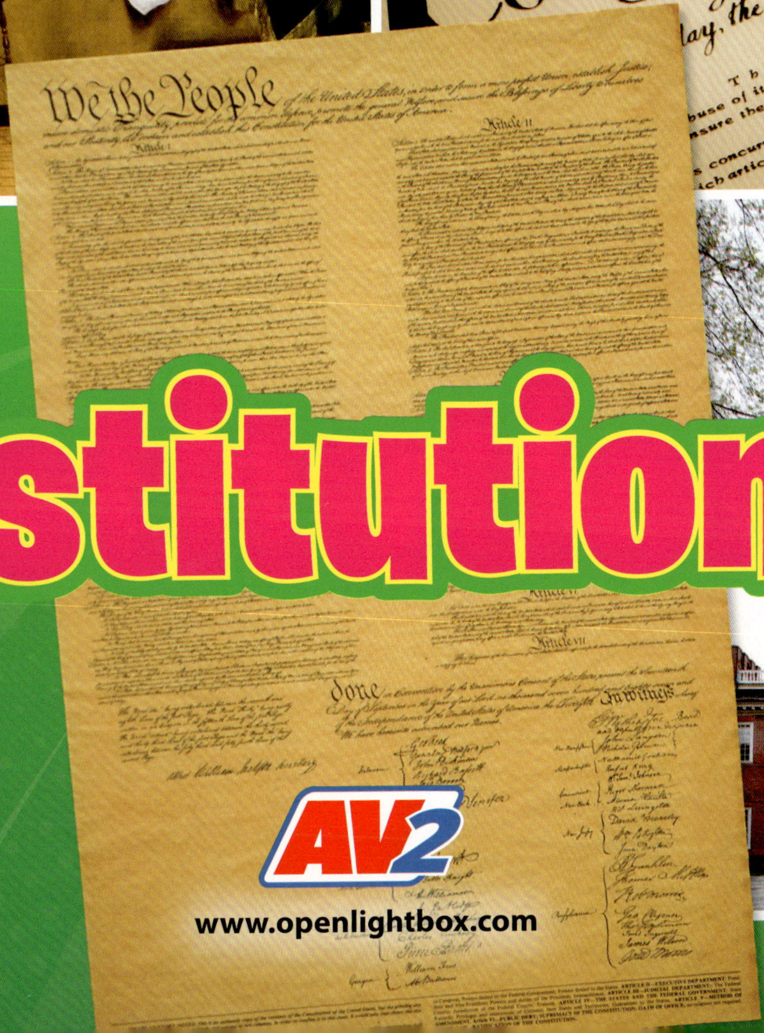

Linda Hopkins

AV2
www.openlightbox.com

AV2

Step 1
Go to **www.openlightbox.com**

Step 2
Enter this unique code
AIBLCP7IA

Step 3
Explore your interactive eBook!

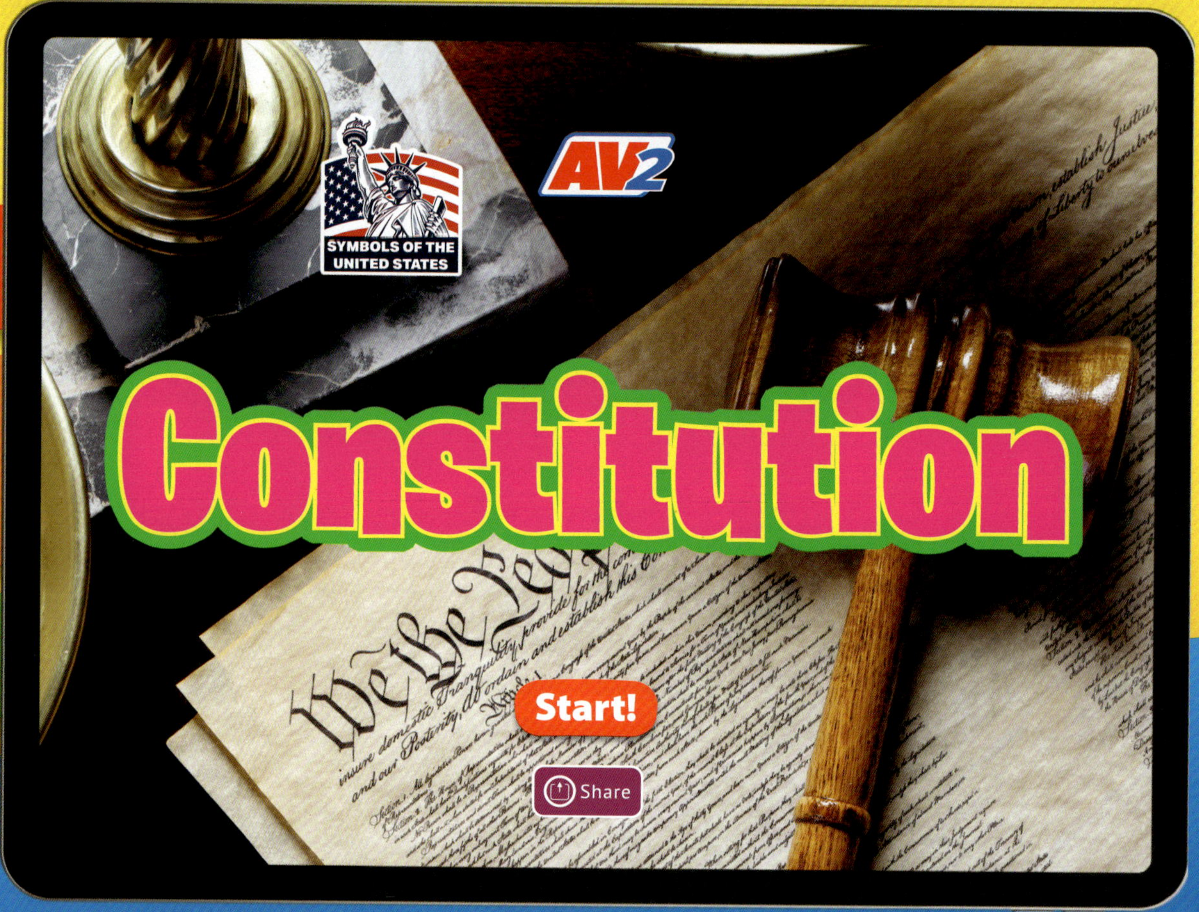

Your interactive eBook comes with...

AV2 is optimized for use on any device

Read

Audio
Listen to the entire book read aloud

Videos
Watch informative video clips

Weblinks
Gain additional information for research

Try This!
Complete activities and hands-on experiments

Key Words
Study vocabulary, and complete a matching word activity

Quizzes
Test your knowledge

Slideshows
View images and captions

Share
Share titles within your Learning Management System (LMS) or Library Circulation System

Citation
Create bibliographical references following APA, CMOS, and MLA styles

This title is part of our AV2 digital subscription

1-Year Texas Subscription
ISBN 978-1-5105-8659-8

Access hundreds of AV2 titles with our digital subscription.
Sign up for a FREE trial at **www.openlightbox.com/trial**

The digital components of this book are guaranteed to stay active for at least five years from the date of publication.

Rows 3-15: Ch 3, turn; 3 dc in first sc, ★ skip next 3 dc and next ch-2, (sc, ch 2, 3 dc) in next sc; repeat from ★ across to last 4 dc, skip next 3 dc, sc in last dc; at end of Row 15, finish off.

WINGS

LONG WING (Make 2)

Row 1: With Black, ch 21; sc in second ch from hook and in each ch across: 20 sc.

Rows 2 and 3: Ch 2, turn; dc in first st and in each st across.

Edging (Right side): Ch 1, turn; sc in each dc across; work 6 sc evenly spaced across end of rows; working in free loops of beginning ch, sc in each ch across; work 6 sc evenly spaced across end of rows; join with slip st in first sc, finish off.

MEDIUM WING (Make 2)

Row 1: With Black, ch 16; sc in second ch from hook and in each ch across: 15 sc.

Rows 2 and 3: Ch 2, turn; dc in first st and in each st across.

Edging (Right side): Ch 1, turn; sc in each dc across; work 6 sc evenly spaced across end of rows; working in free loops of beginning ch, sc in each ch across; work 6 sc evenly spaced across end of rows; join with slip st in first sc, finish off.

SHORT WING (Make 2)

Row 1: With Black, ch 13; sc in second ch from hook and in each ch across: 12 sc.

Rows 2 and 3: Ch 2, turn; dc in first st and in each st across.

Edging (Right side): Ch 1, turn; sc in each dc across; work 6 sc evenly spaced across end of rows; working in free loops of beginning ch, sc in each ch across; work 6 sc evenly spaced across end of rows; join with slip st in first sc, finish off.

EAR HORNS (Make 2)

With Really Red, ch 7.

Row 1 (Right side): Sc in second ch from hook and in each ch across: 6 sc.

Note: Mark Row 1 as **right** side.

Row 2: Ch 1, turn; skip first sc, sc in next 3 sc, skip next sc, sc in last sc: 4 sc.

Row 3: Ch 1, turn; skip first sc, sc in next sc, skip next sc, sc in last sc: 3 sc.

Instructions continued on page 35.

FANCY **FLAMINGO** EASY

Finished Measurement:
Approx. 7" wide x 18" high (18 cm x 46 cm)

MATERIALS
Deborah Norville Everyday™ Soft Worsted Prints (100% acrylic) MEDIUM 4
[3.5 ounces, 180 yards (100 grams, 165 meters) per skein]:
ED200-04 Cotton Candy - 1 skein
Deborah Norville Everyday™ Soft Worsted Solids (100% acrylic) MEDIUM 4
[4 ounces, 203 yards (114 grams, 185 meters) per skein]:
ED100-12 Black - 1 skein
Crochet hook, size G (4 mm) **or** size needed for gauge
Polyester stuffing
12 mm buttons for eyes - 2
Yarn needle

Note: If toy is intended for children under 3 years old, we recommend embroidering the eyes.

GAUGE: 8 sc and 9 rows = 2" (5 cm)

Gauge Swatch: 2" (5 cm) square
Row 1: Ch 9; sc in second ch from hook and in each ch across: 8 sc.
Rows 2-9: Ch 1, turn; sc in each sc across.
Finish off.

STITCH GUIDE

DECREASE
Pull up a loop in each of next 2 sc, YO and draw through all 3 loops on hook **(counts as one sc)**.

HEAD, NECK, & BODY

With Cotton Candy and beginning at top of Head, ch 2.

Rnd 1 (Right side)**:** 6 Sc in second ch from hook; do **not** join, place marker *(see Markers, page 39)*.

Rnd 2: 2 Sc in each sc around: 12 sc.

Rnd 3: (Sc in next sc, 2 sc in next sc) around: 18 sc.

Rnd 4: Sc in each sc around.

Rnd 5: (Sc in next 2 sc, 2 sc in next sc) around: 24 sc.

Rnd 6: (Sc in next 3 sc, 2 sc in next sc) around: 30 sc.

Rnd 7: Sc in each sc around.

Rnd 8: (Sc in next 4 sc, 2 sc in next sc) around: 36 sc.

Rnds 9-15: Sc in each sc around.

Rnd 16: (Sc in next 4 sc, decrease) around: 30 sc.

Rnd 17: Decrease around: 15 sc.

Rnds 18-30: Sc in each sc around.

Rnd 31: 2 Sc in each sc around: 30 sc.

Stuff Head and Neck.

Rnd 32: Sc in each sc around.

Rnd 33: Sc in next 12 sc, 2 hdc in next sc, 2 dc in next 4 sc, 2 hdc in next sc, sc in next 12 sc: 36 sts.

Rnd 34: (Sc in next 5 sts, 2 sc in next st) around: 42 sc.

Rnd 35: (Sc in next 6 sc, 2 sc in next sc) around: 48 sc.

Rnd 36: (Sc in next 7 sc, 2 sc in next sc) around: 54 sc.

Rnds 37 and 38: Sc in each sc around.

Rnd 39: Sc in next 21 sc, decrease 6 times, sc in next 21 sc: 48 sc.

Rnd 40: Sc in next 18 sc, decrease 6 times, sc in next 18 sc: 42 sc.

Rnd 41: Sc in each sc around.

Rnd 42: (Sc in next 5 sc, decrease) around: 36 sc.

Rnd 43: Sc in each sc around.

Rnd 44: (Sc in next 4 sc, decrease) around: 30 sc.

Rnd 45: (Sc in next 3 sc, decrease) around: 24 sc.

Stuff Body.

Rnd 46: (Sc in next 2 sc, decrease) around: 18 sc.

Rnd 47: (Sc in next sc, decrease) around; finish off leaving an 8" (20.5 cm) end for sewing: 12 sc.

Finish stuffing; matching sts, sew opening closed.

BEAK

With Black, ch 2.

Rnd 1 (Right side)**:** 6 Sc in second ch from hook; do **not** join, place marker.

Rnd 2: (Sc in next 2 sc, 2 sc in next sc) around: 8 sc.

Rnds 3 and 4: Sc in each sc around.

Rnd 5: 2 Sc in each of next 2 sc, sc in next sc, decrease twice, sc in next sc: 8 sc.

Rnd 6: Sc in each sc around.

Rnd 7: (Sc in next 3 sc, 2 sc in next sc) around: 10 sc.

Rnd 8: (Sc in next 4 sc, 2 sc in next sc) around: 12 sc.

Rnds 9-11: Sc in each sc around; at end of Rnd 11, finish off leaving a long end for sewing.

Stuff Beak and sew in place. Sew on eyes.

WING (Make 2)

With Cotton Candy, ch 4.

Row 1: Sc in second ch from hook and each ch across: 3 sc.

Row 2: Ch 1, turn; 2 sc in each sc across: 6 sc.

Row 3: Ch 1, turn; sc in each sc across.

Instructions continued on page 32.

FANCY FLAMINGO

Continued from page 31.

Row 4: Ch 1, turn; sc in first 2 sc, 2 sc in each of next 2 sc, sc in last 2 sc: 8 sc.

Row 5: Ch 1, turn; (hdc, dc) in first sc, ★ (dc, hdc) in next sc, ch 1, (slip st, ch 1, hdc, dc) in next sc; repeat from ★ 2 times **more**, (dc, hdc, ch 1, slip st) in last sc; finish off.

Sew Wings to side of Body.

LONG TAIL FEATHERS (Make 6)

With Cotton Candy, ch 10.

Rnd 1 (Right side)**:** Sc in second ch from hook and in next ch, hdc in next 3 chs, dc in next 3 chs, 5 dc in last ch; working in free loops of beginning ch ***(Fig. 2b, page 39)***, dc in next 3 chs, hdc in next 3 chs, sc in next 2 chs; finish off leaving a 6" (15 cm) end for sewing.

Sew Long Tail Feathers to top of Body in 2 rows of 3 feathers each.

SHORT TAIL FEATHERS (Make 3)

With Cotton Candy, ch 7.

Rnd 1 (Right side)**:** Sc in second ch from hook, hdc in next 2 chs, dc in next 2 chs, 5 dc in last ch; working in free loops of beginning ch, dc in next 2 chs, hdc in next 2 chs, sc in next ch; finish off leaving a 6" (15 cm) end for sewing.

Sew Short Tail Feathers to top of Body in front of Long Tail Feathers.

LEG (Make 2)

With Black and beginning at foot, ch 2.

Rnd 1 (Right side)**:** 6 Sc in second ch from hook; do **not** join, place marker.

Rnd 2: 2 Sc in each sc around: 12 sc.

Rnd 3: (Sc in next sc, 2 sc in next sc) around: 18 sc.

Rnd 4: (Sc in next 2 sc, 2 sc in next sc) around: 24 sc.

Rnd 5: Working in Back Loops Only ***(Fig. 1, page 39)***, (sc in next 2 sc, decrease) around: 18 sc.

Rnd 6: Working in both loops, (sc in next sc, decrease) around: 12 sc.

Rnd 7: Sc in each sc around.

Rnd 8: (Sc in next sc, decrease) around: 8 sc.

Rnds 9-39: Sc in each sc around; at end of Rnd 39, finish off leaving a long end for sewing.

Do **not** stuff. Sew Legs in place.

Sew eyes in place.

Design by Michele Wilcox.

BEST FRIENDS: HIPPO & RHINO

Continued from page 25.

FINISHING

Sew Head to Body.

EAR (Make 2)

Row 1: With Lagoon, ch 2; 5 sc in second ch from hook.

Row 2: Ch 1 turn; sc in first 2 sc, 2 sc in next sc, sc in last 2 sc; finish off leaving a 6" (15 cm) end for sewing: 6 sc.

Thread yarn needle with end and sew first and last sc on Row 2 together. With same end, sew Ear to top of Head.

NOSE SHAPING

Thread yarn needle with an 8" (20.5 cm) strand of Lagoon. Working between Rnds 6 and 7 of Head and beginning 6 sts to left of center, run a strand of yarn through Head, ending 6 sts to right of center. Thread yarn through same sts once **more**. Pull ends to create nostril indentations. Secure ends.

With Black, embroider a straight stitch smile ***(Fig. 8, page 40)***.

Design by Michele Wilcox. ●

RHINO

Finished Measurement:
Approx. 12" long x 8" high (30.5 cm x 20.5 cm)

MATERIALS

Deborah Norville Everyday™ Soft Worsted Prints (100% acrylic) MEDIUM 4
[3.5 ounces, 180 yards (100 grams, 165 meters) per skein]:
ED200-09 Beach - 2 skeins
Deborah Norville Everyday™ Soft Worsted Solids (100% acrylic) MEDIUM 4
[4 ounces, 203 yards (114 grams, 185 meters) per skein]:
ED100-12 Black - small amount
Crochet hook size G (4 mm) **or** size needed for gauge
Polyester stuffing
9 mm Black animal eyes - 2
Yarn needle

Note: If toy is intended for children under 3 years old, we recommend embroidering the eyes.

GAUGE: 8 sc and 9 rows = 2" (5 cm)

Gauge Swatch: 2" (5 cm) square
Row 1: Ch 9; sc in second ch from hook and in each ch across: 8 sc.
Rows 2-9: Ch 1, turn; sc in each sc across.
Finish off.

RHINO

With Beach, work same as Hippo Head, Body, Legs, and Finishing.

LARGE HORN

With Beach, ch 2.

Rnd 1 (Right side)**:** 6 Sc in second ch from hook; do **not** join, place marker.

Rnd 2: Sc in each sc around.

Rnd 3: (Sc in next 2 sc, 2 sc in next sc) around: 8 sc.

Rnd 4: (Sc in next sc, 2 sc in next sc) around: 12 sc.

Rnd 5: Sc in each sc around.

Rnd 6: Decrease 3 times, 2 sc in each of next 6 sc: 15 sc.

Rnd 7: Sc in each sc around.

Rnd 8: Decrease 3 times, sc in next sc, 2 sc in each of next 7 sc, sc in next sc: 19 sc.

Rnd 9: Sc in each sc around; finish off leaving a long end for sewing.

Stuff Horn and sew in place.

SMALL HORN

Rnds 1-6: Work same as Large Horn; finish off leaving a long end for sewng: 15 sc.

Stuff Horn and sew in place.

Design by Michele Wilcox. ●

CAT NAP PILLOW

Continued from page 27.

Row 8: Ch 1, turn; sc in each sc across; finish off.

Sew end of rows together; stuff Ear lightly. Sew Ears to top of Head.

TAIL

Row 1: With Parrot, ch 2; 6 sc in second ch from hook.

Row 2 (Right side)**:** Ch 1, turn; 2 sc in each sc across: 12 sc.

Note: Mark Row 2 as **right** side.

Row 3: Ch 1, turn; sc in first sc, 2 sc in next sc, (sc in next sc, 2 sc in next sc) across: 18 sc.

Rows 4-26: Ch 1, turn; sc in each sc across; at end of Row 26, finish off.

Sew end of rows together; stuff Tail lightly. Sew Tail to back of Pillow Body.

LEG (Make 4)

With Parrot, ch 2.

Row 1: 6 Sc in second ch from hook.

Row 2 (Right side)**:** Ch 1, turn; 2 sc in each sc across: 12 sc.

Note: Mark Row 2 as **right** side.

Row 3: Ch 1, turn; sc in first sc, 2 sc in next sc, (sc in next sc, 2 sc in next sc) across: 18 sc.

Row 4: Ch 1, turn; sc in first 2 sc, 2 sc in next sc, (sc in next 2 sc, 2 sc in next sc) across: 24 sc.

Row 5: Ch 1, turn; sc in first 3 sc, 2 sc in next sc, (sc in next 3 sc, 2 sc in next sc) across: 30 sc.

Rows 6-18: Ch 1, turn; sc in each sc across; at end of Row 18, finish off.

Sew end of rows together; stuff Leg lightly. Sew Legs in place over corners of Pillow Body.

TAB

With Parrot, ch 13.

Row 1: Sc in second ch from hook and each ch across: 12 sc.

Rows 2-14: Ch 1, turn; sc in each sc across.

Row 15: Ch 1, turn; sc in first 5 sc, ch 2, skip next 2 sc (buttonhole), sc in last 5 sc: 10 sc and 2 chs.

Row 16: Ch 1, turn; sc in each sc and in each ch across: 12 sc.

Row 17: Ch 1, turn; sc in first sc, decrease, sc in next 6 sc, decrease, sc in last sc: 10 sc.

Row 18: Ch 1, turn; sc in first sc, decrease, sc in next 4 sc, decrease, sc in last sc: 8 sc.

Row 19: Ch 1, turn; sc in first sc, decrease, sc in next 2 sc, decrease, sc in last sc: 6 sc.

Edging (Right side)**:** Ch 1, turn; sc evenly around entire Tab, working 3 sc in each corner; join with slip st to first sc, finish off.

Sew base of Tab (Row 1) to top of Pillow Body, centered between left Legs and 1" (2.5 cm) above side seam.

FINISHING

With Black, embroider satin stitch nose ***(Fig. 7, page 40)*** and straight stitch mouth and whiskers ***(Fig. 8, page 40)***.

Sew eyes in place.

Sew button to top of Pillow Body, centered between right Legs and 1" (2.5 cm) above side seam.

Design by Michele Wilcox.

A REAL HOOT
Continued from page 29.

Row 4: Ch 1, skip first sc, sc in last 2 sc; finish off: 2 sc.

Sew end of rows together.

EYES (Make 2)
With White, ch 2.

Rnd 1: 6 Sc in second ch from hook; do **not** join, place marker.

Rnd 2: 2 Sc in each sc around: 12 sc.

Rnd 3: (Sc in next sc, 2 sc in next sc) around: 18 sc.

Rnd 4: (Sc in next 2 sc, 2 sc in next sc) around: 24 sc.

Rnd 5: Sc in each sc around; finish off.

EYEBALL (Make 2)
Rnd 1: With Black, ch 2; 6 sc in second ch from hook; join with slip st to first sc, finish off leaving a long end for sewing.

Sew one Eyeball to the center of the right side of each Eye.

BEAK
With Black, ch 6.

Row 1 (Right side)**:** Sc in second ch from hook and in each ch across: 5 sc.

Note: Mark Row 1 as **right** side.

Row 2: Ch 1, turn; sc in first sc, (skip next sc, sc in next sc) twice: 3 sc.

Row 3: Ch 1, turn; sc in first sc, skip next sc, sc in last sc; finish off: 2 sc.

Sew end of rows together.

FEET (Make 4)
With Black, ch 10.

Row 1 (Right side)**:** Sc in second ch from hook and in each ch across: 9 sc.

Row 2: Ch 1, turn; sc in each sc across.

Claws: Ch 6, dc in third ch from hook and in next 3 chs, skip first 2 sc, ★ sc in next sc, ch 6, dc in third ch from hook and in next 3 chs, skip next 2 sc; repeat from ★ once **more**, slip st in last sc; finish off.

With **wrong** sides together, sew 2 Feet together. Repeat with remaining 2 Feet.

FINISHING
Stuff the Body of the Owl. Pin the Feet in place inside the bottom edge of the Body; sew bottom seam.

Sew the eyes to face. Sew Beak and Ear Horns to the head.

Sew the Ruffle Feathers around the neck of the Owl. With **right** sides facing up, stack the Medium and Short Wings on the Long Wing, overlapping slightly. Center Wings on side of body and sew in place at neck. Repeat on second side.

Design by Sharon Mann.

SOFT STACKING RINGS

EASY

Finished Height: Approx. 8 1/2" (21.5 cm)

MATERIALS

Deborah Norville Everyday™
Soft Worsted Solids (100% acrylic) MEDIUM 4
[4 ounces, 203 yards (114 grams, 185 meters) per skein]:
- ED100-11 Chocolate - 1 skein
- ED100-09 Royal Blue - 1 skein
- ED100-07 Really Red - 1 skein
- ED100-10 Aubergine - 1 skein
- ED100-08 Pine Green - 1 skein

Crochet hook size G (4 mm) **or** size needed for gauge
Polyester stuffing
Yarn needle

GAUGE: 8 sc and 9 rows = 2" (2 cm)

Gauge Swatch: 2" (5 cm) square
Ch 9.
Work same as Ring 1 Rows 1-9: 8 sc.
Finish off.

RINGS

RING 1

With Chocolate, ch 37.

Row 1 (Right side)**:** Sc in second ch from hook and in each ch across: 36 sc.

Note: Loop a short piece of yarn around any stitch to mark Row 1 as **right** side.

Rows 2-13: Ch 1, turn; sc in each sc across; at end of Row 13, finish off.

RING 2

With Royal Blue, ch 34.

Row 1 (Right side)**:** Sc in second ch from hook and in each ch across: 33 sc.

Note: Mark Row 1 as **right** side.

Rows 2-13: Ch 1, turn; sc in each sc across; at end of Row 13, finish off.

RING 3

With Really Red, ch 31.

Row 1 (Right side)**:** Sc in second ch from hook and in each ch across: 30 sc.

Note: Mark Row 1 as **right** side.

Rows 2-11: Ch 1, turn; sc in each sc across; at end of Row 11, finish off.

RING 4

With Aubergine, ch 28.

Row 1 (Right side)**:** Sc in second ch from hook and in each ch across: 27 sc.

Note: Mark Row 1 as **right** side.

Rows 2-11: Ch 1, turn; sc in each sc across; at end of Row 11, finish off.

RING 5

With Pine Green, ch 25.

Row 1 (Right side)**:** Sc in second ch from hook and in each ch across: 24 sc.

Note: Mark Row 1 as **right** side.

Rows 2-9: Ch 1, turn; sc in each sc across; at end of Row 9, finish off.

RING POST

With Really Red, ch 4; join with slip st to form a ring.

Rnd 1: 6 Sc in ring; do **not** join, place marker ***(see Markers, page 39)***.

Rnd 2: 2 Sc in each sc around: 12 sc.

Rnds 3-5: Sc in each sc around.

Rnd 6: Sc in each sc around, changing to Pine Green in last sc ***(Fig. 3a, page 39)***.

Rnds 7-9: Sc in each sc around.

Rnd 10: Sc in each sc around, changing to Aubergine in last sc.

Rnd 11: Sc in each sc around.

Rnd 12: (Sc in next 3 sc, 2 sc in next sc) around: 15 sc.

Rnds 13 and 14: Sc in each sc around.

Rnd 15: Sc in each sc around, changing to Really Red in last sc.

Rnds 16-20: Sc in each sc around.

Rnd 21: (Sc in next 4 sc, 2 sc in next sc) around, changing to Royal Blue in last sc: 18 sc.

Rnds 22-27: Sc in each sc around.

Rnd 28: Sc in each sc around, changing to Chocolate in last sc.

Rnds 29-35: Sc in each sc around.

Rnd 36: Sc in each sc around; slip st in next sc, finish off.

POST BOTTOM

With Chocolate, ch 4; join with slip st to form a ring.

Rnd 1 (Right side)**:** 6 Sc in ring; do **not** join, place marker.

Rnd 2: 2 Sc in each sc around: 12 sc.

Rnd 3: (Sc in next sc, 2 sc in next sc) around: 18 sc.

Rnd 4: (Sc in next 2 sc, 2 sc in next sc) around; finish off: 24 sc.

BASE RING

With Pine Green, ch 41.

Row 1 (Right side)**:** Sc in second ch from hook and in each ch across: 40 sc.

Rows 3-13: Ch 1, turn; sc in each sc across; at end of Row 13, finish off.

FINISHING

Rings: Fold Ring in half lengthwise with **wrong** sides together, sew beginning ch to last row, lightly stuffing before closing.
Wrap the tube to form a ring and sew ends together.

Repeat with remaining rings.

Stuff the Ring Post and sew the Post Bottom to the back loops ***(Fig. 1, page 39)*** of the last rnd of Ring Post.
Sew the Base Ring to the bottom of the post.

Stack the Rings onto the post.

Design by Sharon Mann. ●

GENERAL INSTRUCTIONS

ABBREVIATIONS

BPdc	Back Post double crochet(s)
CC	Contrasting Color
ch(s)	chain(s)
cm	centimeters
dc	double crochet(s)
FPdc	Front Post double crochet(s)
FPtr	Front Post treble crochet(s)
fhdc	foundation half double crochet(s)
fsc	foundation single crochet(s)
hdc	half double crochet(s)
Ldc	Linked double crochet(s)
MC	Main Color
mm	millimeters
Rnd(s)	Round(s)
sc	single crochet(s)
sp(s)	space(s)
st(s)	stitch(es)
tr	treble crochet(s)
YO	yarn over

★ — work instructions following ★ as many **more** times as indicated in addition to the first time.

( ) or [ ] — work enclosed instructions **as many** times as specified by the number immediately following **or** work all enclosed instructions in the stitch or space indicated **or** contains explanatory remarks.

colon (:) — the number(s) given after a colon at the end of a row or round denote(s) the number of stitches or spaces you should have on that row or round.

Yarn Weight Symbol & Names	LACE 0	SUPER FINE 1	FINE 2	LIGHT 3	MEDIUM 4	BULKY 5	SUPER BULKY 6
Type of Yarns in Category	Fingering, 10-count crochet thread	Sock, Fingering Baby	Sport, Baby	DK, Light Worsted	Worsted, Afghan, Aran	Chunky, Craft, Rug	Bulky, Roving
Crochet Gauge* Ranges in Single Crochet to 4" (10 cm)	32-42 double crochets**	21-32 sts	16-20 sts	12-17 sts	11-14 sts	8-11 sts	5-9 sts
Advised Hook Size Range	Steel*** 6,7,8 Regular hook B-1	B-1 to E-4	E-4 to 7	7 to I-9	I-9 to K-10.5	K-10.5 to M-13	M-13 and larger

*GUIDELINES ONLY: The chart above reflects the most commonly used gauges and hook sizes for specific yarn categories.

** Lace weight yarns are usually crocheted on larger-size hooks to create lacy openwork patterns. Accordingly, a gauge range is difficult to determine. Always follow the gauge stated in your pattern.

*** Steel crochet hooks are sized differently from regular hooks–the higher the number the smaller the hook, which is the reverse of regular hook sizing.

CROCHET TERMINOLOGY		
UNITED STATES		INTERNATIONAL
slip stitch (slip st)	=	single crochet (sc)
single crochet (sc)	=	double crochet (dc)
half double crochet (hdc)	=	half treble crochet (htr)
double crochet (dc)	=	treble crochet(tr)
treble crochet (tr)	=	double treble crochet (dtr)
double treble crochet (dtr)	=	triple treble crochet (ttr)
triple treble crochet (tr tr)	=	quadruple treble crochet (qtr)
skip	=	miss

BEGINNER	Projects for first-time crocheters using basic stitches. Minimal shaping.
EASY	Projects using yarn with basic stitches, repetitive stitch patterns, simple color changes, and simple shaping and finishing.
INTERMEDIATE	Projects using a variety of techniques, such as basic lace patterns or color patterns, mid-level shaping and finishing.
EXPERIENCED	Projects with intricate stitch patterns, techniques and dimension, such as non-repeating patterns, multi-color techniques, fine threads, small hooks, detailed shaping and refined finishing.

CROCHET HOOKS															
U.S.	B-1	C-2	D-3	E-4	F-5	G-6	H-8	I-9	J-10	K-10½	L-11	M/N-13	N/P-15	P/Q	Q	S
Metric - mm	2.25	2.75	3.25	3.5	3.75	4	5	5.5	6	6.5	8	9	10	15	16	19

GAUGE
Exact gauge is **essential** for proper size. Before beginning your project, make the sample swatch given in the individual instructions in the yarn and hook specified. After completing the swatch, measure it, counting your stitches and rows or rounds carefully. If your swatch is larger or smaller than specified, **make another, changing hook size to get the correct gauge**. Keep trying until you find the size hook that will give you the specified gauge.

JOINING WITH SC
When instructed to join with a sc, begin with a slip knot on the hook. Insert the hook in the stitch or space indicated, YO and pull up a loop, YO and draw through both loops on hook.

MARKERS
Markers are used to help distinguish the beginning of each round being worked. Place a 2" (5 cm) scrap piece of yarn before the first stitch of each round, moving the marker after each round is complete.

BACK OR FRONT LOOP ONLY
Work only in loop(s) indicated by arrow ***(Fig. 1)***.

Fig. 1

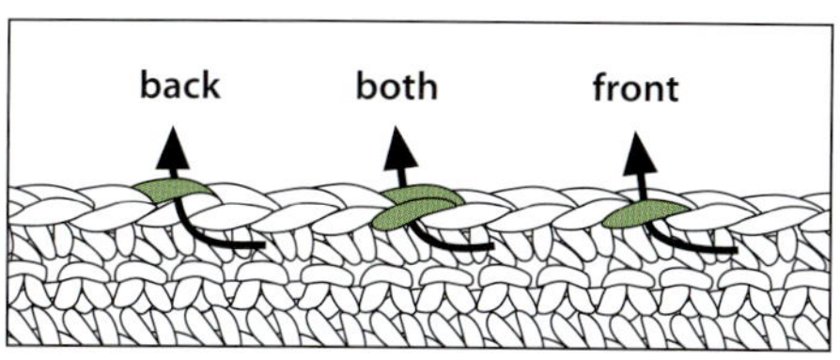

FREE LOOPS
After working in Back or Front Loops Only on a row or round, there will be a ridge of unused loops. These are called the free loops. Later, when instructed to work in the free loops of the same row or round, work in these loops ***(Fig. 2a)***.

When instructed to work in free loops of a chain, work in loop indicated by arrow ***(Fig. 2b)***.

Fig. 2a

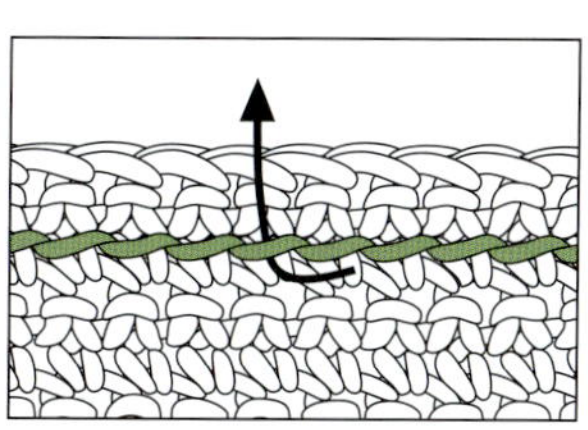

Fig. 2b

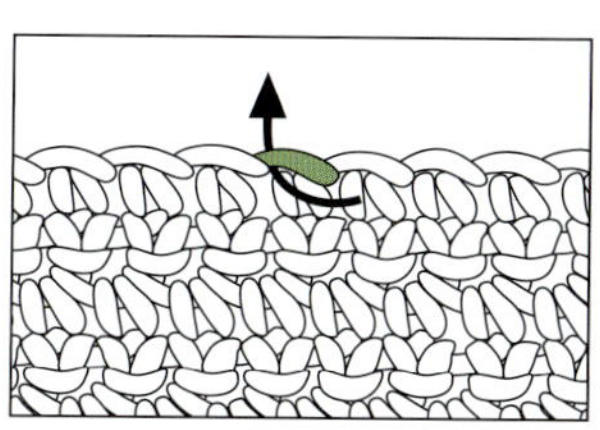

CHANGING COLORS
Work the last stitch to within one step of completion, hook new yarn ***(Figs. 3a-c)*** and draw through all loops on hook. Cut old yarn and work over both ends unless otherwise instructed.

Fig. 3a

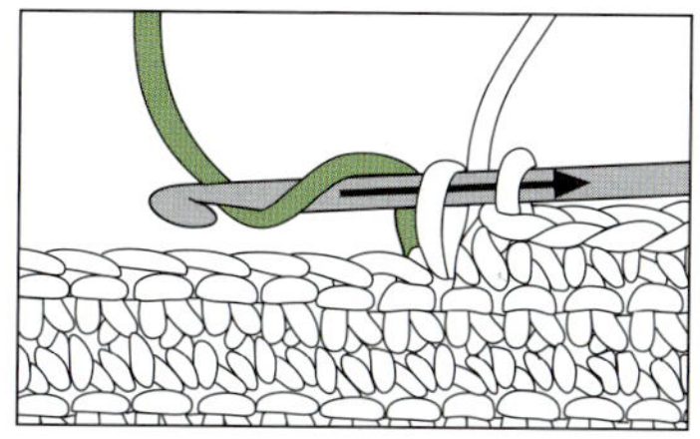

Fig. 3b

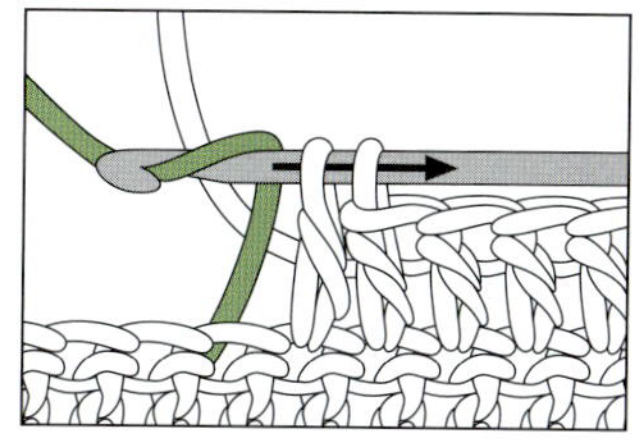

Fig. 3c

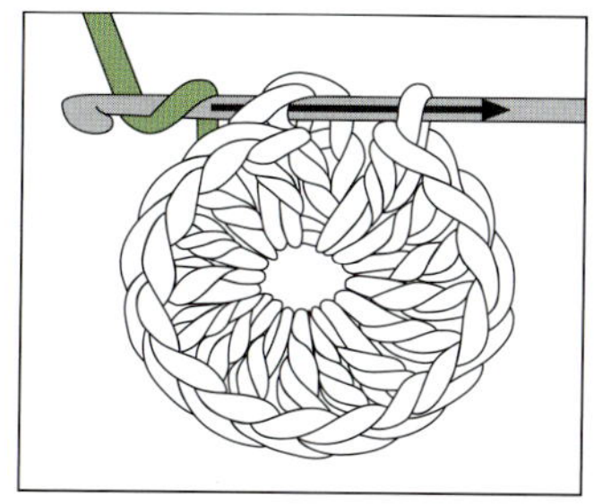

POST STITCH
Work around the post of stitch indicated, inserting hook in direction of arrow ***(Fig. 4)***.

Fig. 4

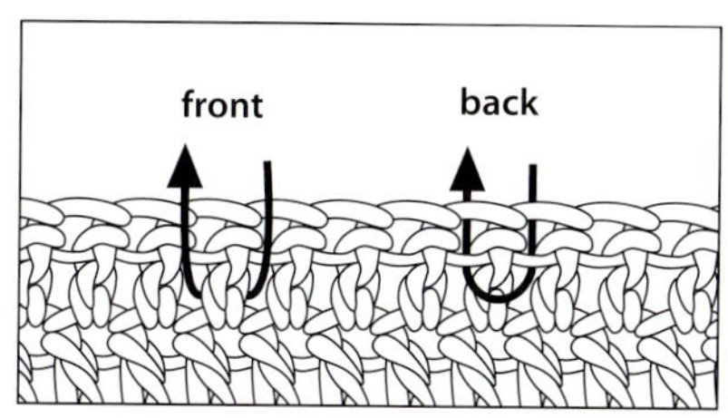

WORKING IN A SPACE BEFORE A STITCH

When instructed to work in a space before a stitch or in spaces between stitches, insert hook in space indicated by arrow *(Fig. 5)*.

Fig. 5

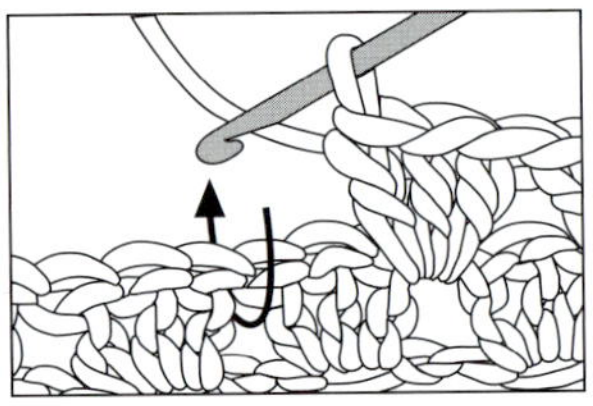

WHIPSTITCH

With **wrong** sides together, sew through both pieces once to secure the beginning of the seam, leaving an ample yarn end to weave in later. Insert the needle from **front** to **back** through **both** loops on **both** pieces *(Fig. 6)*. Bring the needle around and insert it from **front** to **back** through next loops of both pieces. Continue across in this manner, keeping the sewing yarn fairly loose.

Fig. 6

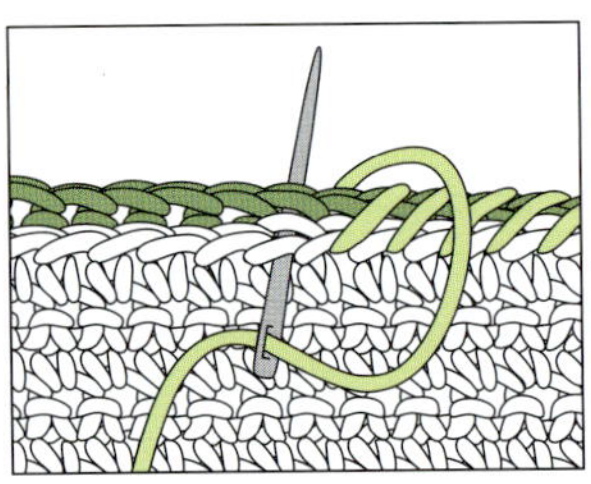

SATIN STITCH

Satin stitch is a series of straight stitches worked side-by-side so they touch but do not overlap. Come up at odd numbers and go down at even numbers *(Fig. 7)*.

Fig. 7

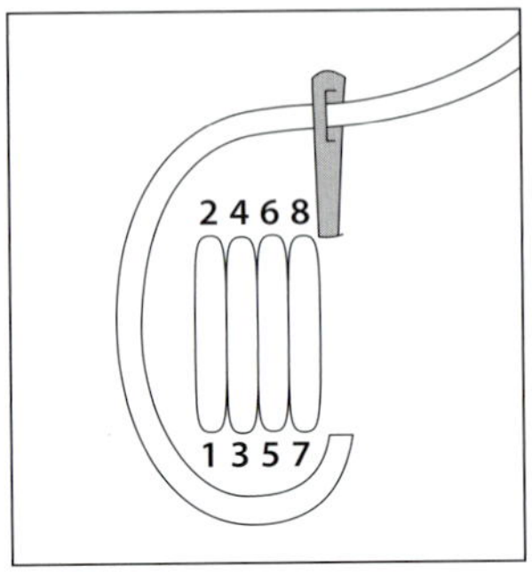

STRAIGHT STITCH

Straight stitch is just what the name implies, a single, straight stitch. Come up at 1 and go down at 2 *(Fig. 8)*.

Fig. 8

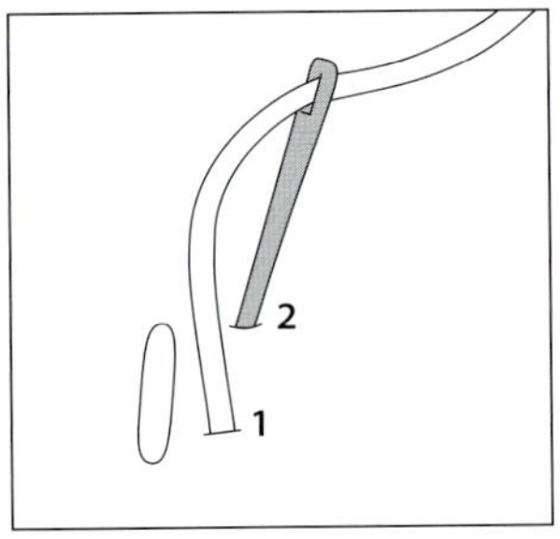

Production Team: Writers/Technical Editors - Joan Beebe and Linda A. Daley; Editorial Writer - Susan McManus Johnson; Senior Graphic Artist - Lora Puls; Graphic Artist - Becca Snider; Photo Stylists - Sondra Daniel and Cora Holdaway; and Photographers - Jason Masters and Ken West.

SYMBOLS OF THE UNITED STATES

Constitution

CONTENTS

THE HIGHEST LAW

The U.S. Constitution is the highest law in the United States.

It is a set of rules about how the country is run.

The **U.S. Constitution** is one of the world's **oldest national constitutions** still in use.

ARTICLES OF CONFEDERATION

The first constitution of the United States was called the Articles of Confederation.

It became the law on March 1, 1781.

In **1781**, the **United States** had only **13 states**.

Drafting the Articles of Confederation
York Town, Pennsylvania
1777
13c
USA

8

CONSTITUTIONAL CONVENTION

People from different states later met in Philadelphia, Pennsylvania. They wrote a new constitution.

The meeting was called the Constitutional Convention.

"WE THE PEOPLE"

The new Constitution was signed on September 17, 1787.

Its authors wanted everyone to know that the people of the United States were making their own rules.

We the People
of the United States

A LIVING DOCUMENT

The U.S. Constitution is a living document. This means that it can be changed.

Changes to the Constitution are known as amendments.

The original **Constitution** is kept at the **National Archives** in **Washington, DC.**

THE FIRST AMENDMENT

The First Amendment is one of the most important changes to the Constitution.

It protects the freedom of speech and religion.

We the People
1st Amendment
law respecting an establishment of
freedom of speech, or of the press; or
for a redress of

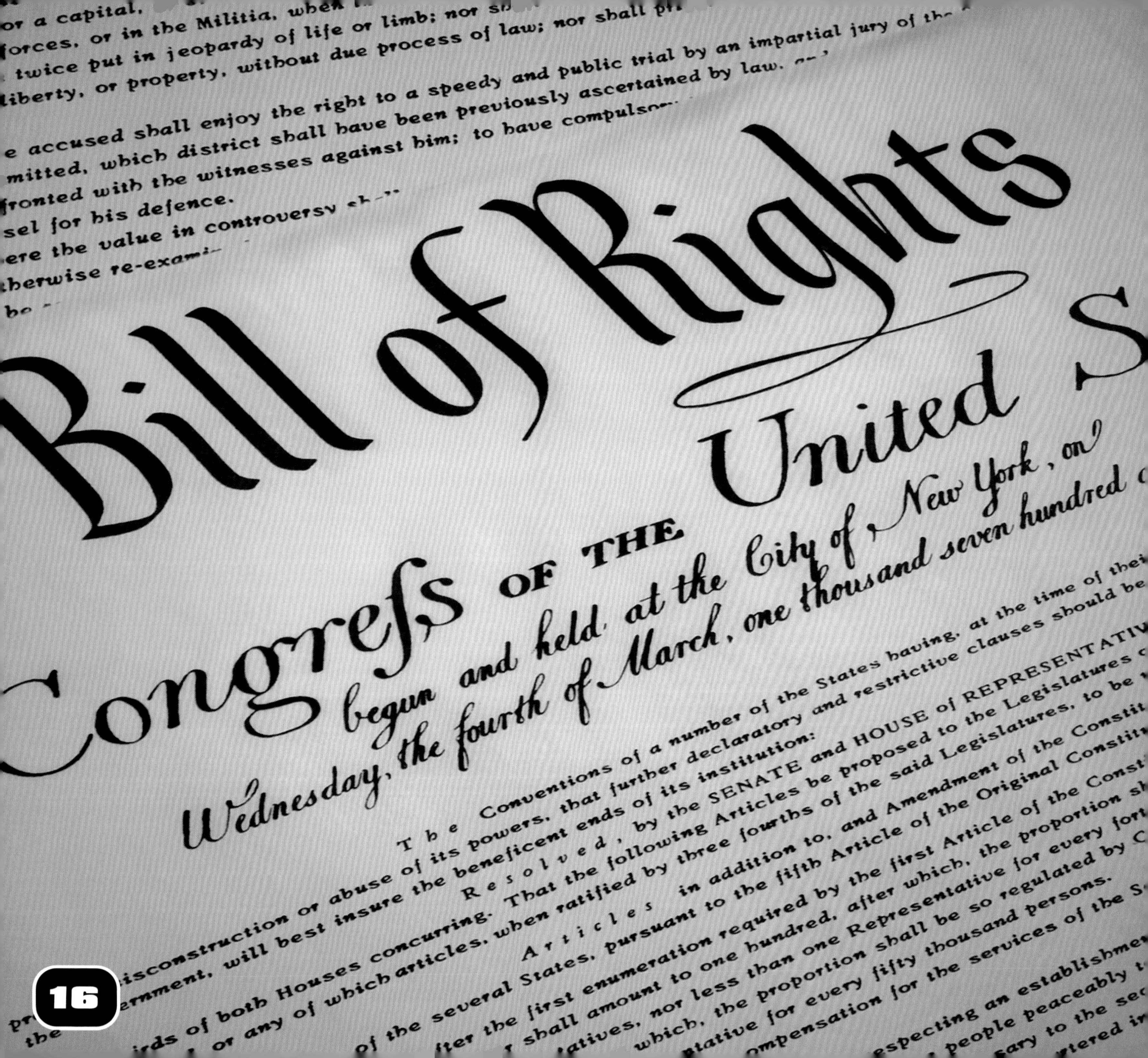

or a capital,
forces, or in the Militia, when
twice put in jeopardy of life or limb; nor sh
liberty, or property, without due process of law; nor shall
accused shall enjoy the right to a speedy and public trial by an impartial jury of the
mitted, which district shall have been previously ascertained by law,
fronted with the witnesses against him; to have compulso
sel for his defence.
ere the value in controversy
herwise re-exami
Bill of Rights
United S
Congress OF THE
begun and held at the City of New York, on
Wednesday, the fourth of March, one thousand seven hundred
The Conventions of a number of the States having, at the time of thei
isconstruction or abuse of its powers, that further declaratory and restrictive clauses should be
ernment, will best insure the beneficent ends of its institution:
Resolved, by the SENATE and HOUSE of REPRESENTATIV
of both Houses concurring. That the following Articles be proposed to the Legislatures o
or any of which articles, when ratified by three fourths of the said Legislatures, to be
Articles in addition to, and Amendment of the Constit
of the several States, pursuant to the fifth Article of the Original Constit
ter the first enumeration required by the first Article of the Const
shall amount to one hundred, after which, the proportion sh
atives, nor less than one Representative for every fort
which, the proportion shall be so regulated by C
ative for every fifty thousand persons.
ompensation for the services of the S
especting an establishme
people peaceably t
sary to the se

BILL OF RIGHTS

Together, the first 10 changes made to the Constitution were called the Bill of Rights.

The Bill of Rights protects the rights of each American.

RESPECTING THE CONSTITUTION

People who serve in the U.S. government must promise to follow the Constitution.

This is called an oath of office.

THE STATE OF TEXAS
GOVERNOR

THE CONSTITUTION TODAY

Constitution Week is held from September 17 to 23 each year.

It celebrates the signing of the Constitution.

Constitution Week was **first celebrated** in **1956**.

CONSTITUTION FACTS

These pages provide detailed information that expands on the interesting facts found in the book. They are intended to be used by adults as a learning support to help young readers round out their knowledge of each icon in the *Symbols of the United States* series.

Pages 4–5

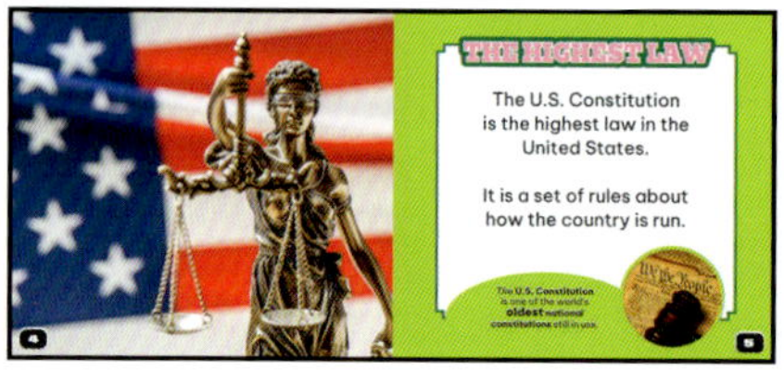

The Highest Law

A national constitution defines the basic principles that govern how a country is run. The Constitution of the United States outlines a system of federalism. This means that the federal government shares power with the states. The Constitution also establishes a separation of powers, dividing the government into three branches. These are the executive, legislative, and judicial branches.

Pages 6–7

Articles of Confederation

The Articles of Confederation was the first constitution of the United States. It was written during the American Revolutionary War, which the United States fought from April 19, 1775, to September 3, 1783, to gain its independence from Great Britain. The Continental Congress adopted the Articles of Confederation on November 15, 1777. However, this constitution did not come into effect until March 1, 1781.

Pages 8–9

Constitutional Convention

Weaknesses in the Articles of Confederation became obvious very quickly. It severely limited the power of the federal government, which could not collect taxes, call up an army, or pass laws without the agreement of state governments. Representatives from each of the 13 states, except Rhode Island, met at the Constitutional Convention to improve the Articles of Confederation. The meeting lasted four months and resulted in the creation of a whole new Constitution.

Pages 10–11

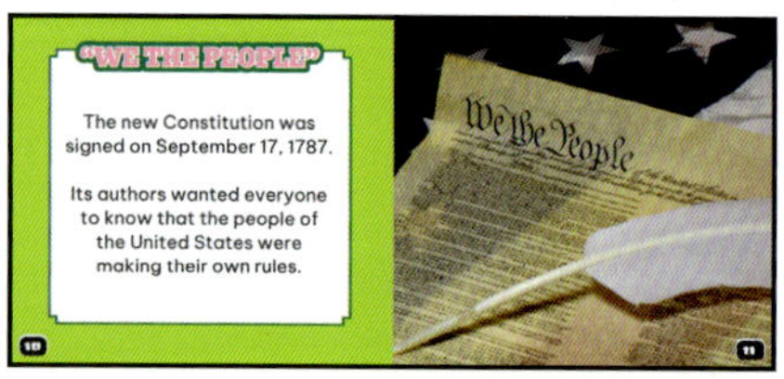

"We the People"

After winning the American Revolutionary War, the people of the newly formed United States of America wanted to make it clear that they were no longer ruled by the king of England or any other monarch. Instead, they would rule themselves. The U.S. Constitution aptly begins with the phrase, "We the People of the United States." Citizens were given the right to vote, and a democracy was established.

Pages 12–13

A Living Document

The Founding Fathers of the United States recognized that amendments to the Constitution could be needed as the country grew and changed. Article V of the Constitution outlines the process of making an amendment. Each amendment must be approved by two thirds of the House of Representatives, two thirds of the Senate, and three quarters of the state legislatures. To date, 27 amendments have been made to the Constitution, with the most recent passing in 1992.

Pages 14–15

The First Amendment

The First Amendment to the Constitution grants all U.S. citizens freedom of speech and religion. Citizens have the right to assemble, protest, and petition the government. This amendment also protects the freedom of the press.

Pages 16–17

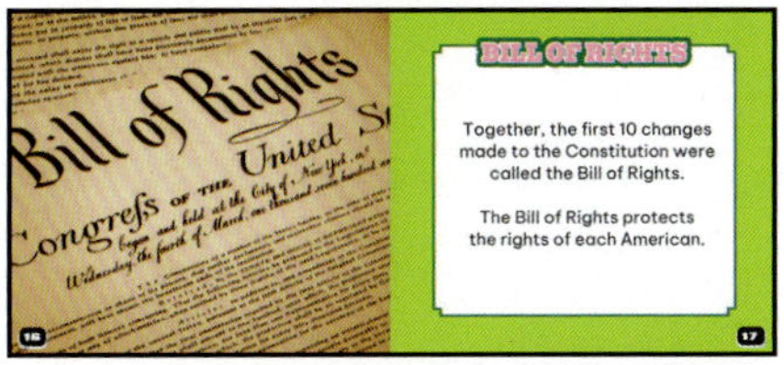

Bill of Rights

The first 10 amendments, or the Bill of Rights, came into effect in 1791. The Bill of Rights establishes the freedoms to which all U.S. citizens are entitled. These include the right to bear arms and the right to a fair trial. The Bill of Rights also protects the rights of individual states.

Pages 18–19

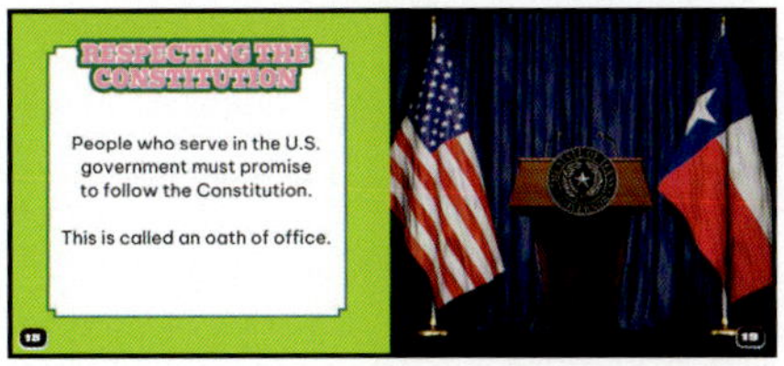

Respecting the Constitution

All elected government officials in the United States must take an oath of office. The first sentence of their oath begins, "I do solemnly swear that I will support and defend the Constitution of the United States." Civil servants, military personnel, lawyers, and new citizens must also swear oaths to support and uphold the Constitution.

Pages 20–21

The Constitution Today

Each year, Constitution Week is observed from September 17 to 23. This resulted from a petition to Congress by the Daughters of the American Revolution (DAR), a non-profit organization. President Dwight D. Eisenhower signed Constitution Week into law on August 29, 1956. The week begins with Constitution Day, which usually falls on September 17. During this week, schools often encourage students to reflect on the rights and responsibilities of all citizens.

KEY WORDS

Research has shown that as much as 65 percent of all written material published in English is made up of 300 words. These 300 words cannot be taught using pictures or learned by sounding them out. They must be recognized by sight. This book contains 55 common sight words to help young readers improve their reading fluency and comprehension. This book also teaches young readers several important content words, such as proper nouns. These words are paired with pictures to aid in learning and improve understanding.

Page	Sight Words First Appearance
5	a, about, country, how, in, is, it, of, one, run, set, states, still, the, use, world
6	first, had, on, only, was
9	different, from, later, new, people, they
10	its, know, own, that, their, to, we, were
13	are, as, at, be, can, changes, means, this
14	and, important, most
17	American, each, made, rights, together
18	an, must, who
21	year

Page	Content Words First Appearance
5	law, rules, United States, U.S. Constitution
6	Articles of Confederation
9	Constitutional Convention, meeting, Pennsylvania, Philadelphia
10	authors
13	amendments, document, National Archives, Washington, DC
14	First Amendment, freedom, religion, speech
17	Bill of Rights
18	government, oath of office
21	Constitution Week

Published by Lightbox Learning Inc.
276 5th Avenue, Suite 704 #917
New York, NY 10001
Website: www.openlightbox.com

Library of Congress Control Number: 2024939043

ISBN 978-1-5105-8119-7 (hardcover)
ISBN 979-8-8745-1492-1 (softcover)
ISBN 978-1-5105-8375-7 (static multi-user eBook)
ISBN 978-1-5105-8377-1 (interactive multi-user eBook)

Printed in Guangzhou, China
1 2 3 4 5 6 7 8 9 0 28 27 26 25 24

072024
100923

Project Coordinator: Priyanka Das
Designer: Terry Paulhus
Layout: Jean Faye Rodriguez

The publisher acknowledges Alamy and Getty Images as the primary image suppliers for this title.